Budapest

Budapest

Text by Péter Dobai

Corvina

On the cover: The Danube embankment, Buda, with the Matthias Church
and the Hilton Hotel on Castle Hill
On the back cover: The Parliament building
On the title-page: View from Gellért Hill

Photographs by

Cover: Zsolt Szabóky
Back cover: Albert Kozák (IPV)
Title-page: Csaba Raffael (MTI)

Lóránt Bérczi 8, 17, 62
M. Chrushkova 73 (IPV)
Lajos Czeizing 72
Tamás Diner 36, 51, 52, 84
Endre Domonkos 54
János Eifert 7, 25, 35, 38
István Faragó 11, 18, 22, 31, 43, 47, 50, 56, 58, 64, 80
György Gara 5, 15, 16, 39, 40, 41, 45, 78
László Gyarmati 12, 21 (IPV), 27, 28, 69, 81
András Hász 4, 60, 63, 79
Károly Hemző 2, 6, 10 (IPV), 14, 19 (IPV), 23, 30, 32, 33, 34, 37, 44, 59, 61, 74, 76, 87, 88
János Huschit 82
Péter Korniss 42, 48, 71, 86, 89
András Marton 13
András Nagy 24, 26, 66, 68
Károly Német 49
Árpád Patyi 90
András Surányi 20, 65, 67
Zsolt Szabóky 1, 3, 9, 29, 46, 70, 75, 77, 85
Zoltán Szalay 57 (IPV)
János Szerencsés 83
Gyula Tahin 55
László Török 53 (IPV)

Translated by Judith E. Sollosy and Lidia Dobos
Design by Erzsébet Szabados
© Péter Dobai, 1986
ISBN 963 13 2277 7
Printed in Hungary, 1986
Kossuth Printing House, Budapest
CO 2438-h-8688

An old port, an old haven, an old royal free borough whose rich past reaches back to the distant centuries of the Roman Empire, Budapest lies on two banks of the Danube, the most beautiful river in Europe. And although this city is located deep within the heart of Europe, the Danube connects it, like so many others, with the sea. Originally, Budapest was three separate towns—Óbuda, Buda and Pest, which were united in 1873, and which, through the years, became a truly major capital city. But even before the Romans came, the caves of Buda, its forests rich in game and vegetation, the thermal springs of its gently rolling hills sloping down to the Danube attracted many settlers. Later the Roman legions camped by the Danube, on the site of today's Óbuda, and soon their camp grounds developed into Aquincum, the capital of the province of Lower Pannonia. Its massive walls, however, were razed to the ground by the resurgent waves of the Great Migrations and were consequently buried under the mud of Danubian floods. Luckily, the 20th century has uncovered the ancient routes and atriums, the

foundations of the Roman castrums, so that today Aquincum stands on the bank of the Danube as a song of praise to the past. The ruins of that most important Roman-age establishment, the amphitheatre, whose arena was filled over a thousand years ago by the motley tents of the conquering Magyars, also stand today as a robust reminder of Antique culture.

During the Middle Ages, the status of Buda as a city grew: it won the rights of a port and of holding regional fairs from the kings. In the wake of the terrible ravages of the Mongol Invasion, the construction of the Castle of Buda (1247) was begun, whose stormy history has defined the lives and fates of the merchants, craftsmen, grape-growers and fruit merchants who settled behind its bastions and below its walls in increasingly greater numbers. However, after a rich Renaissance flowering, the city and country fell under Turkish rule for a hundred and fifty years, and was wrenched out of the mainstream of European development. The united Christian armies succeeded in recapturing the Castle only in 1686, at the

time of the decline of the Turkish empire. Most of the medieval houses perished during the long siege, and afterwards, the district took on its baroque appearance which still characterizes it today. The two towns of Buda and Pest were united in the energetic and optimistic 19th century, the age of the steamship and the railway, a marriage as much hallmarked by the dynamic appearance of new bridges spanning the Danube as by the new, monumental cityscape.

From all parts of the country and beyond, the main thoroughfares and railways converged on the new city.

Yet Budapest had to undergo another rebirth after the Second World War. In the spring of 1945, when the last canons had fallen silent, Budapest was a city of the homeless and of dismal ruins, a city without bridges. But it was rebuilt once more—a triumph of determination over the passion for destruction. Today the bridges, those lovely bridges of Pest and Buda, arch over the river once again, and new districts, new housing estates bear witness to peace.

Along all great rivers, great cities rise; Budapest is the city of the Danube, of its bridges and islands, indivisible from it, living and breathing along with its heaving waters which surge towards the south. Indeed, Budapest's most breathtaking monument is the Danube itself. No architect or stonecutter has ever conceived a more magnificent edifice than this 'edifice' of water which had stood here long before man ever settled its shores, and whose water had given sustenance and a means of transportation to a long row of successive generations. Budapest's most beautiful and best-known buildings, old and new alike, were all built on the banks of the Danube or overlooking its waters from the surrounding hillsides. On its eastern bank, in Pest, stand the building of the Parliament, the Hungarian Academy of Sciences, a row of modern luxury hotels, the Inner City Parish Church whose history goes back to the Middle Ages, and the neo-Renaissance edifice of the Karl Marx University of Economics. In Buda, on the western bank of the river, lie the old thermal baths and modern pools, the villas on Rózsadomb

(Rose Hill), the famed Fishermen's Bastion, the Matthias Church, the Hilton Hotel and the Royal Palace on Castle Hill, the Citadella, the impressive Secessionist Gellért Hotel and Baths on Gellért Hill, and further to the south, the University of Technology, and many apartment and public buildings—all facing the Danube, the mighty river which carries the legend of Budapest down to the sea.

In fact, the most pleasant way of approaching Budapest is by boat on the Danube. On the way from up north, the passangers can see the Basilica rising high above the town of Esztergom, the ruins of the royal castle of Visegrád, and the most breathtaking sight of all, the Danube Bend, followed by the cathedral of Vác and the towers of this bishop's town—and along the banks, there stand a gentle chain of hills, Szentendre's colourful rooftops with their touch of the Mediterranean. Drifting past dark green, seemingly deserted islands, the traveller will then see the Roman Banks, a popular beach with boathouses and rows of poplars, and finally, the misty silhouettes of the towers and

domes of Budapest itself. The city has two hearts: Buda on its hills and Pest on its plains. Someone looking down at Budapest from Gellért Hill, the Fishermen's Bastion or the lookout tower of János Hill sees *one* city, but he who gets to know Budapest learns to love *two* towns. Buda lies on the heights, the sides and terraces of the hills and mountains, the *home* of the past.

Facing it from the east is Pest, much larger than Buda in territory, with its new housing projects seemingly hovering over the flat, distant horizon and its massive industrial districts on the outskirts. In contrast to the intimacy of romantic, Baroque-style Buda, its dimensions are truly on a grand scale. In fact, Pest too is old, ancient, and has retained vestiges of this past, though not as openly as Buda. The former town walls and gates, the marble remains of ancient, dried-out wells can still be seen, though, in the courtyards and firewalls of the Inner City, sometimes in quite good condition.

As long as this city stands, Buda will always remain the royal city,

and Pest the bourgeois town, the alliance of the two blessed by the bridges over the Danube. Buda has retained the historical and architectural monuments due to a royal seat—the Castle, forts, palaces, monasteries and churches that belong to the past. With its larger proportions, Pest bears the stamps of bourgeois virtues and of conscious city planning. Its boulevards, avenues and roundabouts belong to the age of industrial development. Buda offers a more picturesque sight, while Pest is more practical and massive.

Buda's rich and effective, sometimes modest architectural remains force man to accomodate himself to past centuries, while the fate of Pest is dictated by the present. Though Pest has long ago gained ascendancy with its two operas, many theatres, sports stadiums and academies of the fine and performing arts, of the humanities and sciences, Buda has kept the best of itself: historical monuments which, for us today, are becoming more and more precious, and the prerogative of seigniority with its more ancient walls and their hidden secrets, its prerogative of a sense of painful recall and of nostalgia.

A man walking around Budapest becomes acquainted with a different city in Buda, and a different city in Pest. But his walk in either part of the capital takes him along the banks of the same river, which finally unites Buda and Pest into the one and only Budapest. Whether he strolls in the Castle District or among the medieval and baroque houses of Buda, captivated by their seemingly purposeless archways, perhaps imagining himself in another century for one illogical instant; whether he walks through the domed Turkish baths below the Castle or wanders around the streets of Pest, where past and present merge and vie for prominence, he is enjoying the sights of an unforgettable city, one he will want to visit again and again, to walk through its Castle area, its Gellért Hill, and to climb the lookout towers on the hills of Buda, from where he can see the great semicircles formed by Buda and Pest, with the Danube, this historical equator of East and West between them.

Péter Dobai

1–2 Roman tombstones
in the Aquincum open-air
museum
3 Aquincum Museum:
the lapidarium
4 Roman mosaic floor in the
Hercules villa
5 Ruins of Aquincum,
capital of the one-time
Roman province of Lower
Pannonia

6 The Southern Round Bastion of the reconstructed medieval castle
7 The palace gardens in the medieval section of Buda Castle
8 The Mace Tower

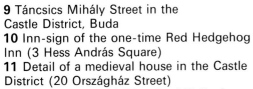

9 Táncsics Mihály Street in the
Castle District, Buda
10 Inn-sign of the one-time Red Hedgehog
Inn (3 Hess András Square)
11 Detail of a medieval house in the Castle
District (20 Országház Street)
12 Wine-cellar at 10 Táncsics Mihály Street

13 Bécsi kapu Square
14 The Hilton Hotel on Hess András Square, which incorporates details from earlier buildings, including this Baroque façade

15 Gothic niches in the gateway of 32 Úri Street
16 Courtyard at 32 Úri Street
17 Lion with coat of arms on the corner of 13 Úri Street
18 Statue of Pallas Athene with the arms of Buda in front of the old Buda Town Hall (2 Szentháromság Square)
19 Courtyard at 13 Dísz Square

20 Balta köz
21 Wrought-iron window grills of the
Baroque mansion at 7 Táncsics Mihály Street
22 Café under arches dating from the 15th
century (14 Tárnok Street)

◁ **23** Gate in the fortified wall of Buda Castle
◁ **24** Castle Hill with the Royal Castle

25 The eastern wing of Buda Castle houses the Hungarian National Gallery. Central staircase
26 Red marble carvings from King Matthias Corvinus' (1458–1490)
Renaissance palace in the Budapest Historical Museum
27 14th-century Gothic statues in the Gothic Hall of Buda Castle. These were discovered in 1974 during the work of reconstruction
28 Matthias Fountain in the courtyard of Buda Castle

29 One of the pinnacles of
the neo-Romanesque
Fishermen's Bastion, with the
Parliament in the background
30 Fishermen's Bastion
—detail
31–32 Street vendor
and street musician on the
Fishermen's Bastion

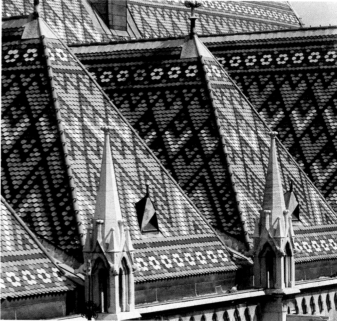

33–34 Matthias Church—details
35 The south door of
Matthias Church
36 Matthias Church

37 Terrace of the Hilton Hotel ▷
38 View of the Buda Hills from
the tower of Matthias Church ▷

39 Steps leading up to Castle Hill
40–41 The Turkish Király Baths in Fő Street
42 Rococo building on Batthyány Square, at one time
the White Cross Inn

43–45 The Danube embankment: a favourite spot to sun yourself or fish
46 Buda and Pest are separated by the Danube. In the foreground: the Royal Castle and the Chain Bridge; in the background: Margaret Bridge and Island

47–52 Old trees, broad lawns and a quiet atmosphere: Margaret Island, Budapest's biggest and finest park

◁**53** The Inner City of Pest

54 Felszabadulás Square and Kossuth Lajos Street
55 The Pest bridgehead of Elizabeth Bridge with the
Inner City Parish Church

56–58 Inner City details: a cherub on the wall of the Franciscan Church; the interior of the Paris Arcades; and the Fountain of the Nereids in front of the Franciscan Church
59 Art Nouveau building on Felszabadulás Square dating from the turn of the century

60–62 Inner City snapshots
63 Kígyó Street—a pedestrian precinct in
the Inner City

64 The 19th-century Danubius Fountain
on Engels Square
65 Vörösmarty Square with Gerbeaud's famous
pastry shop
66 Enjoying light refreshment at Gerbeaud's....
67 .... and on the benches in Vörösmarty Square

◁ **68** Forum Hotel on the Pest embankment and the statue of
József Eötvös, 19th-century novelist and statesman
◁ **69** The Romantic building of the Vigadó, the Municipal
Assembly Rooms

70 The oldest bridge of the city, Chain Bridge was opened in
November 1849
71 Façade of the Hungarian Academy of Sciences

72 Main hall and staircase in the Parliament
73 Arcades of the Parliament
74 The neo-Gothic Parliament

75 Statues of St. Stephen's Basilica, the biggest church in Budapest, with view of Bajcsy-Zsilinszky Street
76–78 Buildings dating from the turn of the century in Rákóczi Street and the Great Boulevard—two of the city's main thoroughfares

79 The 100-year-old Opera House
80 Detail from one of the buildings on
Népköztársaság Road dating from
the late 19th century
80–82 The Opera House—details

83 Népköztársaság Road leads
up to Hősök tere (Heroes' Square)
84 Heroes' Square with the
Millennial Monument
85 The Millennial Monument—
detail

86 City Park Lake
with Vajdahunyad Castle ▷

87 Statue of Anonymus, the chronicler of King Béla III
(1173–1196)
88 Boating on the City Park Lake
89 Gateway to Vajdahunyad Castle

90 The Buda embankment of the Danube ▷